Scientists Look for Patterns and Rules

Wayan James

Rosen REAL READERS

Rosen Classroom™
New York

Things in nature follow certain patterns and rules.
Can you think of an example?
The sun rises and sets each day.

Scientists look for patterns.
It helps them understand how
things work.

A life cycle is a pattern.
A caterpillar hatches.
The caterpillar eats.

It spins a case around itself.
It changes into a butterfly!

Tides follow a pattern, too. The levels of the ocean move up and down every day.

Scientists learned that the moon makes tides happen.

Plants follow a pattern.

A planted seed will grow.

It makes a new plant.

That plant makes seeds.

New plants grow.

A fish has gills.

It needs water to breathe.

People need food, water, and shelter to live.

Words to Know

butterfly

caterpillar

fish

moon

scientist

seeds